KITES

T0014860

APEX

BY CONNOR STRATTON

WWW.APEXEDITIONS.COM

Apex is distributed by North Star Editions:
sales@northstareditions.com | 888-417-0195

Produced for Apex by Red Line Editorial.

Photographs ©: Shutterstock Images, cover (bird), 1 (bird), 4–5, 8, 9, 10–11, 12, 13, 14–15, 16–17, 18–19, 20, 21, 22–23, 24, 24–25, 26–27, 29; Unsplash, cover (background), 1 (background); iStockphoto, 6–7

Library of Congress Control Number: 2021915656

ISBN
978-1-63738-145-8 (hardcover)
978-1-63738-181-6 (paperback)
978-1-63738-252-3 (ebook pdf)
978-1-63738-217-2 (hosted ebook)

Printed in the United States of America
Mankato, MN
012022

NOTE TO PARENTS AND EDUCATORS

Apex books are designed to build literacy skills in striving readers. Exciting, high-interest content attracts and holds readers' attention. The text is carefully leveled to allow students to achieve success quickly. Additional features, such as bolded glossary words for difficult terms, help build comprehension.

TABLE OF CONTENTS

CHAPTER 1

HUNTING ON THE FLY

A swallow-tailed kite soars over a **swamp**. The bird swoops and turns. Its wings stretch out wide.

Swallow-tailed kites live near swamps and rivers in North and South America.

Soon, the kite sees a lizard on a tree branch. The bird **glides** toward the animal. It grabs the lizard and keeps on flying. Its sharp claws grip its **prey**.

Swallow-tailed kites fly close to trees to catch prey. Sometimes they fly in groups.

SMOOTH GLIDERS

Swallow-tailed kites spend most of the day in the air. The birds don't flap their wings very often. Instead, they hold their wings open. Their thin bodies glide smoothly and easily through the air.

The kite carries the lizard to its nest. Two baby birds sit inside. The young kites are hungry. They gobble up the lizard.

Adult swallow-tailed kites mainly eat insects. Young kites eat lizards.

Baby kites have soft, fuzzy feathers.

Swallow-tailed kites and red-tailed hawks are about the same size. But the hawks weigh twice as much.

CHAPTER 2

LIFE IN THE WILD

Kites live all over the world. But they are mostly found in warm places. Many kites live near water or trees.

Red kites can be found in Europe, Africa, and Asia.

Kites often build their nests high in trees. Female kites lay eggs in the nests. Parents care for the babies after they hatch.

Most kites make nests and have babies in spring or summer.

Unlike many kites, black kites tend to live near open areas.

CITY LIFE

Black kites can survive in many **habitats**. They have even **adapted** to live in cities. These birds may perch on telephone poles. Sometimes they steal food from humans!

Many kites **migrate** south during winter. They return north in spring to **breed**. Other kites stay put all year.

Mississippi kites are social. They often hunt, nest, and migrate in large groups.

Mississippi kites fly to tropical areas for the winter. In the spring, they fly north to breed.

CHAPTER 3

LONG TAILS, LONG WINGS

Most kites have small, light bodies. Their wings are long and narrow. These **traits** help kites stay in the air without much effort.

A black kite's wings can be 59 inches (150 cm) across.

Kites have long, narrow tails. Several kinds of kites have forked tails. This tail shape helps kites fly smoothly at low speeds.

A kite's color and tail shape can change as it grows into an adult.

The scissor-tailed kite is known for its forked tail and the black patches on its wings.

Most kites have small heads and narrow beaks. Some kites' beaks are sharply curved. This shape helps the birds tear meat and break shells.

A hook-billed kite's beak can be big or small. The size depends on the type of snail the bird eats.

A snail kite can grab a snail right out of the water.

SNAIL KITES

The snail kite eats only snails. This kite flies above water. Then it swoops down to catch snails. It uses its curved beak to pull snails out of their shells.

CHAPTER 4

HOW KITES HUNT

Kites eat many kinds of animals. Some mainly eat insects. Others hunt small rodents.

Yellow-billed kites catch and eat bats. Termites are another common food.

Red kites and black kites are **scavengers**. They find and eat dead animals and garbage. Brahminy kites do this, too.

By eating animals that have died, red kites can help stop disease from spreading.

Brahminy kites live along coasts in Asia and Australia.

Brahminy kites sometimes steal fish from other birds.

Many kites eat their prey in midair.

Black kites sometimes fly over fires. They catch insects that try to escape the flames.

Most kites glide through the air to hunt. A few types of kites **hover**. Hook-billed kites walk along tree branches to find their food.

PICNIC THIEVES

Red kites sometimes take people's food. These birds look for picnics or outdoor dining. Then they swoop down. Some grab food right as people are about to take a bite!

COMPREHENSION QUESTIONS

Write your answers on a separate piece of paper.

1. Write a sentence describing one way that kites hunt their prey.

2. Would you rather stay in one place all year or migrate back and forth like some kites do? Why?

3. Kites are mostly found in what kinds of places?
   - A. warm places
   - B. cold places
   - C. places with no water

4. How would having small bodies help kites fly with less effort?
   - A. Smaller bodies can have more feathers.
   - B. Smaller bodies take less energy to move.
   - C. Smaller bodies take more energy to move.

5. What does **gobble** mean in this book?

*The young kites are hungry. They **gobble** up the lizard.*

    A. to hold still
    B. to run from
    C. to eat quickly

6. What does **social** mean in this book?

*Mississippi kites are **social**. They often hunt, nest, and migrate in large groups.*

    A. never moving or changing
    B. liking to be alone
    C. liking to be together with others

Answer key on page 32.

GLOSSARY

adapted
Changed to fit a new situation.

breed
To come together to have babies.

glides
Moves smoothly and easily.

habitats
The places where animals normally live.

hover
To stay flying in the air in one spot.

migrate
To move from one part of the world to another.

prey
An animal that is hunted and eaten by another animal.

scavengers
Animals that eat dead animals they did not kill.

swamp
An area of low land covered in water, often with many plants.

traits
Details that set animals apart from others, such as fur color or body shape.

TO LEARN MORE

BOOKS

Hamilton, S. L. *Hawks*. Minneapolis: Abdo Publishing, 2018.

Huddleston, Emma. *How Birds Fly*. Minneapolis: Abdo Publishing, 2021.

Sommer, Nathan. *Kites*. Minneapolis: Bellwether Media, 2019.

ONLINE RESOURCES

Visit **www.apexeditions.com** to find links and resources related to this title.

ABOUT THE AUTHOR

Connor Stratton writes and edits nonfiction children's books. He loves observing birds wherever he goes.

INDEX

Answer Key:
1. Answers will vary; **2.** Answers will vary; **3.** A; **4.** B; **5.** C; **6.** C